CELLS AND

Anita
Ganeri

SYSTEMS

Heinemann

C151853391

KT-558-472

www.heinemann.co.uk
Visit our website to find out more information about Heinemann Library books.

To order:
 Phone 44 (0) 1865 888066
 Send a fax to 44 (0) 1865 314091
 Visit the Heinemann Bookshop at www.heinemann.co.uk to browse our catalogue and order online.

First published in Great Britain by Heinemann Library, Halley Court, Jordan Hill, Oxford OX2 8EJ a division of Reed Educational and Professional Publishing Ltd. Heinemann is a registered trademark of Reed Educational & Professional Publishing Ltd.

OXFORD MELBOURNE AUCKLAND
JOHANNESBURG BLANTYRE GABORONE
IBADAN PORTSMOUTH (NH) USA CHICAGO

Designed by Celia Floyd
Illustrations by Alan Fraser
Originated by Dot Gradations
Printed in Hong Kong/China

ISBN 0 431 10924 9 (hardback)   ISBN 0 431 10931 1 (paperback)
05 04 03 02 01   06 05 04 03 02 01
10 9 8 7 6 5 4 3 2   10 9 8 7 6 5 4 3 2 1

British Library Cataloguing in Publication Data

Ganeri, Anita
  Cells and systems. – (Living things)
  1. Cells – Juvenile literature 2. Cytology – Juvenile literature
  I. Title
  571.6

Acknowledgements

The Publishers would like to thank the following for permission to reproduce photographs:

Action Plus: Glyn Kirk pg.15; *Science Photo Library*: pg.20, Andrew Syred pg.5, pg.11, Eye of Science pg.6, Claude Nuridsany & Marie Perennou pg.6, CNRI pg.7, Dr Jeremy Burgess pg.10, Manfred Kage pg.12, Prof P Motta/Dept of Anatomy/University La Sapienza/Rome pg.13, pg.25, Profs P Motta, PM Andrews, KR Porter & J Vial pg.14, National Cancer Institute pg.16, Manfred Kage pg.19, D Phillips pg.21, Quest pg.23, Don Wong pg.24, Don Fawcett pg.27, Dr Yorgos Nikas pg.28, Neil Bromhall pg.28, L Willatt/East Anglian Genetics Service pg.29.

Cover photograph reproduced with permission of Science Photo Library.

Every effort has been made to contact copyright holders of any material reproduced in this book. Any omissions will be rectified in subsequent printings if notice is given to the Publisher.

Any words appearing in the text in bold, **like this**, are explained in the glossary.

Contents

Introduction

The six books in this series explore the world of living things. *Cells and Systems* looks at the amazing world of plant and animal cells and systems. It explains how groups of cells work together to build every part of a living thing's body.

What are cells?

All living things are made of cells. Cells are like tiny building blocks. They build every part of a living thing's body. Cells do many special jobs such as taking in food, growing, **reproducing** and getting rid of waste. They keep living things alive and in good working order.

Animal cells

An animal cell is like a tiny bag filled with jelly. The cell has a thin skin to hold it together. In the centre of the cell is the **nucleus**. It controls everything that happens inside the cell.

An animal cell.

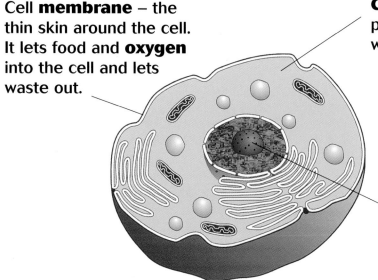

Cell **membrane** – the thin skin around the cell. It lets food and **oxygen** into the cell and lets waste out.

Cytoplasm – the main part of the cell. It is like a watery jelly.

Nucleus – the control centre of the cell. It tells the cell what to do. It divides to make new cells.

Plant cells

Plant cells are very similar to animal cells. But plant cells have three extra features. They have a tough wall made of **cellulose**. They have **chloroplasts** for making food. They have a large **vacuole** filled with cell **sap**.

A plant cell.

Cytoplasm

Nucleus

Cell wall – tough skin around the cell. It holds the cell together.

Vacuole – a large space inside the cell. It is filled with cell sap.

Chloroplasts – tiny discs that contain a green **chemical** called **chlorophyll**. Plants use chlorophyll to make their own food.

How many cells?

Some living things, such as human beings and trees, are made of millions of cells. Other living things have only one cell in their bodies. An amoeba is a tiny, one-celled **organism**. It lives in water. It moves by making its cytoplasm flow along. To make a new amoeba, it simply splits in two.

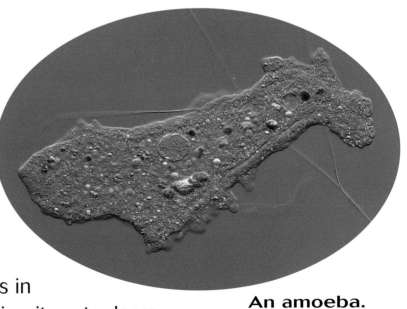

An amoeba.

Cell specialists

Living things are made of many different types of cells. Some cells have special features for doing a particular job. Cells do not work on their own. They are grouped together to build the different parts of a living thing's body.

Special cells

Cells come in different shapes and sizes, depending on the job they do.

- **Nerve** cells – are long and thin for carrying messages all over your body (see page 27).

- Red blood cells – carry **oxygen** around your body. They are doughnut shaped. This gives the cells a large surface for picking up lots of oxygen (see page 16).

- Ciliated cells – these are thin, flat cells that line your air passages (see page 21). They are covered in tiny hairs, called cilia, that trap dirt and **germs**.

- Root-hair cells – these cover a plant's roots. The cells look like hairs and give a large surface for sucking water from the ground (see page 10).

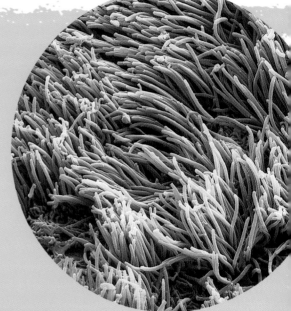

Cilia lining an air passage.

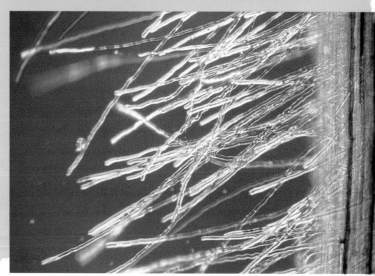

Plant root-hairs.

Cells and systems

Cells work together in groups. Groups of cells make tissues, such as your muscle tissue or bone tissue. Groups of different tissues make organs. Your heart and lungs are organs. Groups of organs work together to make systems, such as your digestive system. It uses organs, such as your stomach and **intestines**.

Life processes

The cells in your body work to keep you alive. Your cells carry out seven life processes. These are:

1 Movement – all living things can move at least part of their bodies.
2 **Respiration** – this is how cells use oxygen to get **energy** from food.
3 Sensitivity – living things sense the world around them.
4 Feeding – living things need food for energy and growth.
5 Excretion – this means getting rid of waste.
6 **Reproduction** – how living things produce young.
7 Growth – all living things grow.

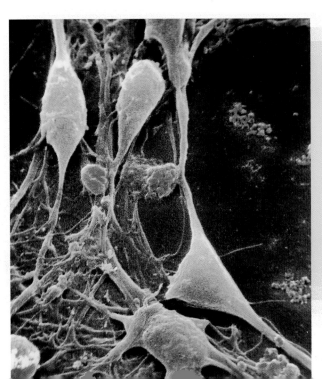

Brain cells.

Did you know?
Some of your brain cells will last a lifetime. But the cells that line your small intestine only live for two to three days. Then new cells are made to replace them.

Plant systems

Some plants only have one cell. Other plants, such as trees, have millions of cells. Some plant cells do special jobs. They make food for the plant, take in water and carry water and food around the plant. Groups of cells make plant tissues, such as xylem and phloem (see page 10). Groups of tissues make plant organs, such as roots, stems and leaves.

Parts of a plant

Flowering plants can be as small as a daisy, or as big as a horse chestnut tree. Here you see the main parts of a flowering plant.

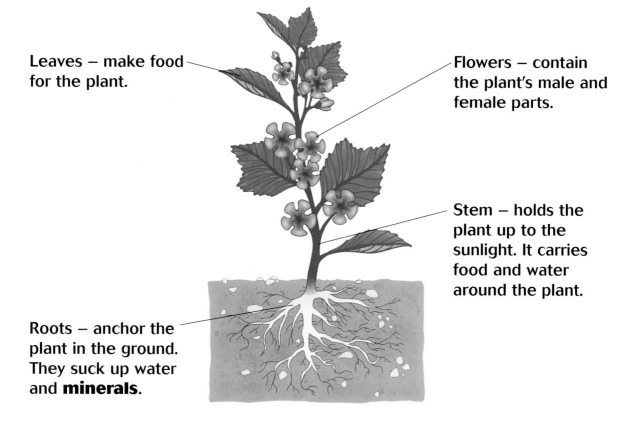

Leaves – make food for the plant.

Flowers – contain the plant's male and female parts.

Stem – holds the plant up to the sunlight. It carries food and water around the plant.

Roots – anchor the plant in the ground. They suck up water and **minerals**.

Making food

All living things need **energy** to survive. The energy comes from food. Green plants make their own food by a process called **photosynthesis**. This happens in the plant's leaves. Inside the leaf cells are **chloroplasts** that contain **chlorophyll**. The chlorophyll uses sunlight to turn **carbon dioxide** from the air and water from the ground into food.

Respiration

Living things use **oxygen** from the air to release energy from food. This is called **respiration**. It happens inside a plant's cells. Plants take in oxygen through their leaves. They give off carbon dioxide as waste.

Flowers and seeds

Flowers contain the plant's male and female cells. The male cells are called **pollen**. The female cells are called **ovules**. For a new plant to grow, the pollen and ovules must join together to make a new cell. The new cell grows into a seed. The seed grows into a new plant.

Inside a leaf

Upper epidermis – the upper skin of the leaf. It is made of a single layer of cells. The cells let sunlight through.

Palisade cells – a layer of tall cells just under the epidermis.

Chloroplasts – tiny discs inside the palisade cells. They contain chlorophyll for making food.

Lower epidermis – the lower skin of the leaf.

Stomata – tiny holes in the leaf. They let water and gases through.

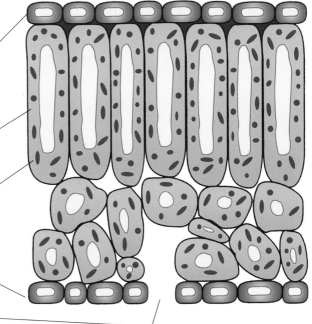

Plant plumbing

Some special cells inside a plant work together to carry food and water around the plant. The plant's roots suck water up from the ground. Then it travels up the stem to the leaves.

Root-hair cells

A plant's roots grow into the ground. The tips of the roots are covered in thousands of tiny tubes called root-hairs. The root-hairs are made from root cells. They grow into the soil and suck up water and **minerals**. Plants have millions of root-hairs on their roots. These help them to take in large amounts of water.

Root-hairs.

Transport system

The roots suck water up. Then the water travels through tiny tubes to the leaves. The tubes are called xylem. Another set of tubes carry **sap** from the leaves to the rest of the plant. These tubes are called phloem. The tubes look like bundles of drinking straws running through the plant's stem.

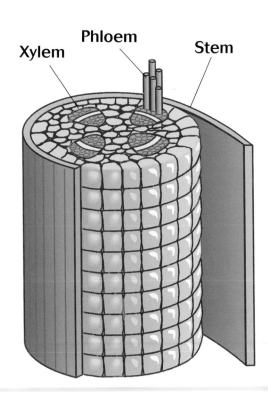

Xylem   Phloem   Stem

Inside a stem.

Plant juices

Sap is a syrupy juice found inside plants. It is a mixture of water and sugary food. It flows around the plant, carrying food from the leaves to every part of the plant. Many insects pierce plant stems to feed on the nourishing sap inside.

Did you know?

A tree trunk is made of wood. The wood is made of old xylem tubes. As the tree grows, the tubes in the centre of the trunk fill up with hard wood. The wood holds the tree up and supports its weight.

Losing water

Plants use some of the water that is drawn up for making food. But most of the water is lost through tiny holes under the plant's leaves. The water **evaporates** into the air. The holes are called stomata. Two sausage-shaped cells open and close the stomata.

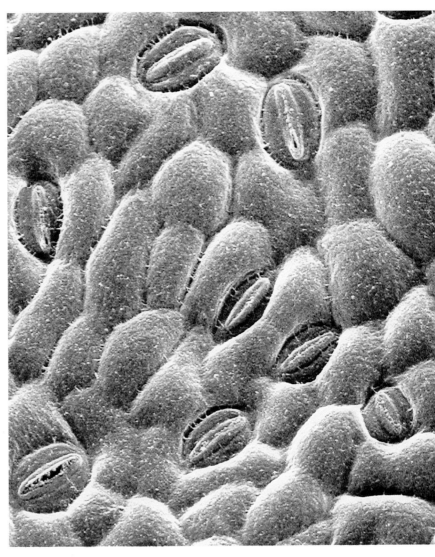

Tiny stomata holes on a leaf.

Bones

Like all living things, your body is made of cells. Your cells make up all the parts of your body. Your body parts work together to make you grow and keep you healthy. Many of your cells do special jobs. Take the bones in your skeleton, for example.

Skeleton support

Your skeleton is made of bones. Bones are a type of tissue that is made of bone cells. Your skeleton has three important jobs to do. Firstly, it holds your body up and gives it its shape. Secondly, it protects your organs from bumps and knocks. Thirdly, your bones work with your muscles so that you can move about (see pages 14).

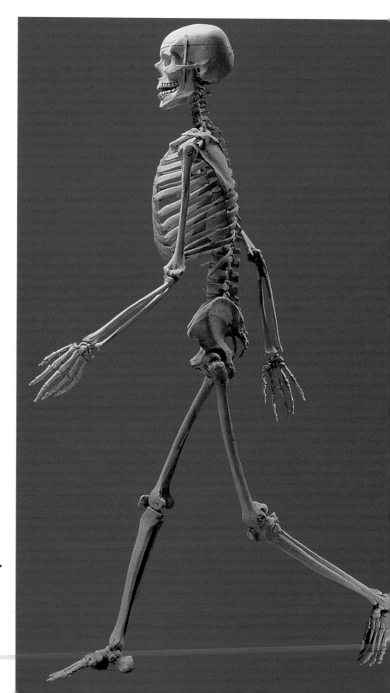

The human skeleton.

Tough bones

The outer part of a bone is hard and tough. It is made of non-living tissue. This makes your bones very strong for supporting your weight and protecting your insides. The inside of a bone is soft and spongy. It is made of living tissue. This makes your bones light for moving about and flexible so that they do not snap or break too easily.

Growing bones

You have more than 200 bones in your skeleton. They come in many shapes and sizes. When you were a baby, some of your cells made gristly **cartilage**. Gradually, the cartilage turned into hard bone. This will carry on happening until you are about 25 years old. Some of the cartilage never turns to bone. You can feel it in the end of your nose and in your earflaps.

Inside a bone.

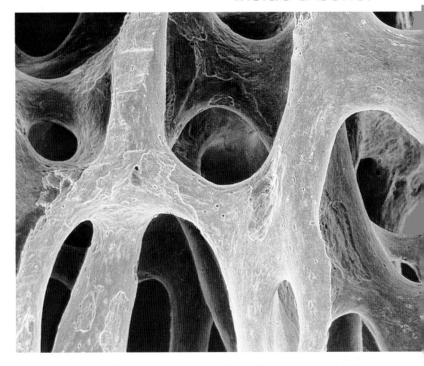

Did you know?
Your bones are covered in a thin, tough coat of living bones cells. If you break a bone, the bone cells grow over the break and join the parts together. You might need a plaster cast to help the bones heal.

Moving muscles

You have hundreds of muscles all over your body. They are under your skin and they make your organs, such as your heart or bladder. Many muscles are attached to bones. They allow you to move about. Your muscles are a type of tissue. The muscles that are fixed to your bones are called stripy muscles. This is because the muscle tissue looks stripy.

Muscle cells

Stripy muscle is made of long, thin cells. The cells are called muscle fibres. The fibres are like stretchy threads. There are more than 2000 fibres inside a big muscle. Each of these fibres is made of even finer threads. The fibres' shape allows them to stretch so that you can move the different parts of your body.

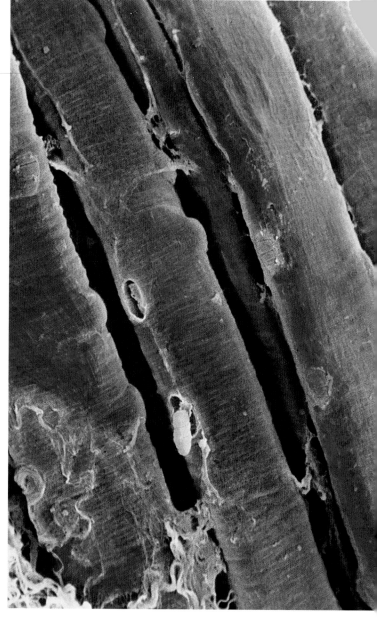

Stripy muscle under a microscope.

How muscles work

Your muscles pull on your bones to make them move. Muscles can only pull and not push. So many of your muscles work in pairs. To bend your elbow, the **biceps** in your upper arm pulls while the **triceps** relaxes. Then the biceps relaxes and the triceps pulls to straighten your arm again. Signals from your brain tell your muscles how and when to make your bones move.

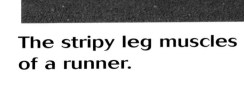

The stripy leg muscles of a runner.

Muscle power

Your muscles need lots of **oxygen** and **energy** to make them work. They get energy from the food you eat and oxygen from the air. Your blood carries the food and oxygen all over your body to your muscle cells.

Did you know?

You have more than 600 muscles in your body. Your biggest muscles are in your bottom and thighs. Your smallest muscles are deep inside your ears. Muscles make up about a third of your body weight.

The circulatory system

Your blood carries **energy** from your food and **oxygen** to all your cells. Otherwise they could not work. The blood travels along tiny tubes called blood vessels. It is pumped along by your heart. Your heart, blood and blood vessels are called your **circulatory** system.

Blood cells

Blood is made of tiny cells floating in a watery liquid called **plasma**. You have about 5 litres of blood inside your body.

- Red blood cells – these carry oxygen around your body. They contain a **chemical** called **haemoglobin**. It turns your blood red. The red blood cells take in oxygen in your lungs, then flow to your heart to be pumped around your body.

- White blood cells – these help your body to fight disease. Some white blood cells eat up harmful **germs**. Other white blood cells stick on to germs and kill them.

- Platelets – these are tiny fragments of cells. They break off larger cells. They help your blood to **clot** so that you do not lose too much blood when you cut yourself.

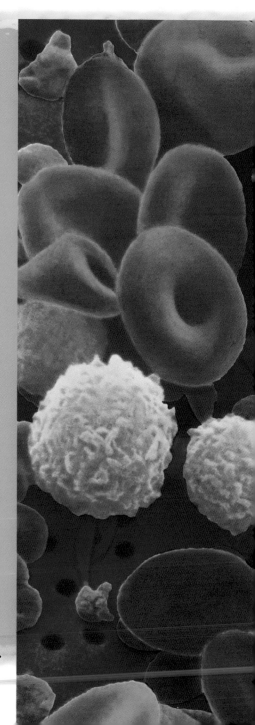

Red blood cells, white blood cells and platelets.

Blood vessels

Blood travels in tubes called blood vessels. There are three different kinds. **Arteries** are strong tubes that carry blood from your heart. They divide into tiny tubes called **capillaries**. The capillaries reach all of your cells. Then they join up again to form bigger tubes called **veins**. The veins carry the blood back to your heart.

The circulatory system.

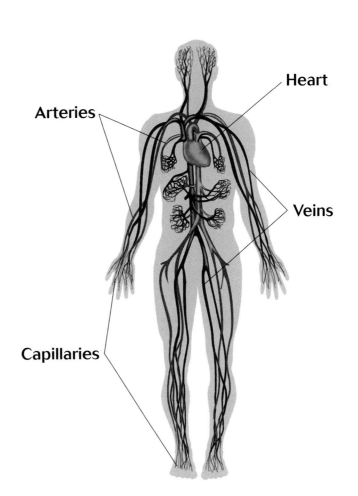

Arteries

Heart

Veins

Capillaries

The heart

Your heart is an organ. It is about the size of your clenched fist and it is made of strong muscle. Your heart works like a pump, pushing blood around your body. Each pump of your heart is called a heartbeat.

Your heart beats about 100,000 times a day, about once every second.

Did you know?

A pin-prick of blood contains 2,500,000 red blood cells, 5000 white blood cells and 250,000 platelets. You have about 30 billion red blood cells in your body.

The digestive system

Everything you do uses **energy**. You get energy from the food you eat. Food also contains the goodness that you need to grow and stay healthy. Feeling hungry is your body's way of telling you that its energy supplies are running low. Your blood carries food around your body. But first the food must be broken down into tiny pieces. This is called **digestion**.

Digesting a meal

1 Your teeth and tongue chew and mash your food. It is mixed with **saliva** to make it easier to swallow.

2 The food goes down your **oesophagus** into your stomach.

3 In your stomach, special juices help dissolve the food. It turns into a thick, creamy mixture like soup.

4 The food is squeezed into your small **intestine**. It is mixed with more juices to break it down.

5 The useful parts of your food seep through your small intestine into your blood.

6 Any waste food goes into your large intestine. It passes out of your body as solids called **faeces**.

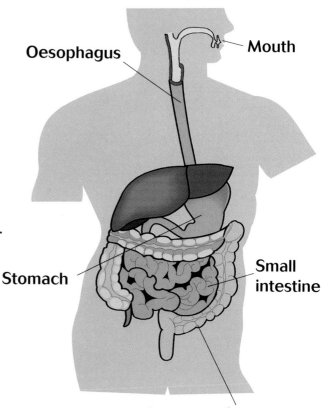

The digestive system.

Mouth

Oesophagus

Stomach

Small intestine

Large intestine

How food gets into your blood

Your small intestine is lined with tiny finger-like spikes called villi. The picture on the right shows you what villi look like under a microscope. The villi give a huge surface area for taking in food.

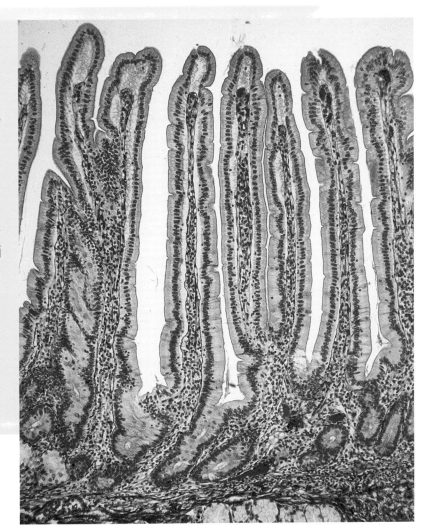

Villi lining the small intestine.

Your teeth

You have two sets of teeth in your lifetime. You grow your first set of 20 teeth by about the age of two. These teeth are called your milk teeth. By the age of six, you start to grow your 32 adult teeth.

Did you know?
Your whole digestive system is about 9 metres long. It takes a meal up to three days to travel all the way through it.

The respiratory syste

Your cells need **oxygen** to make them work. They use this oxygen to release **energy** from the food you eat. You get oxygen from the air when you breathe. The air goes into your two lungs. Your blood carries it from your lungs to all your cells. Your cells make waste water and **carbon dioxide**. Your blood carries these to your lungs to be breathed out. The parts of your body that you use for breathing are called your respiratory system.

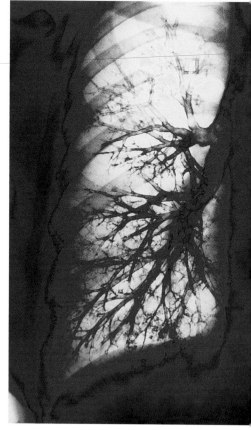

Inside a lung.

Breathing in

When you breathe in, you suck air in through your nose or mouth. The air goes down a long tube in your throat, called the **trachea**. Then the air goes down two shorter tubes, called your **bronchi**, into your lungs. Your chest gets bigger so that your lungs have room to fill with air.

The respiratory system.

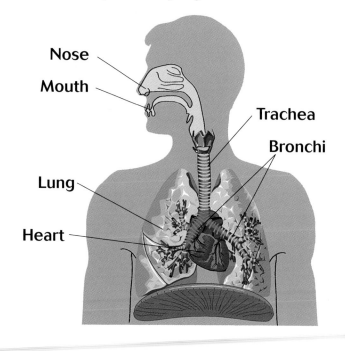

Nose
Mouth
Trachea
Bronchi
Lung
Heart

Gas exchange

Each of your lungs has millions of tiny air sacs, called alveoli. They look like tiny balloons. They are covered in blood vessels. Here oxygen passes from the air you breathe into your blood. Then your blood carries it to your cells. Carbon dioxide passes from your blood into your lungs for breathing out.

Breathing out

When you breathe out, your chest pushes down to squeeze stale air out of your lungs. The air is pushed up the bronchi and up through your throat. Then you breathe it out through your nose or mouth. You breathe in and out all the time, automatically, without having to think.

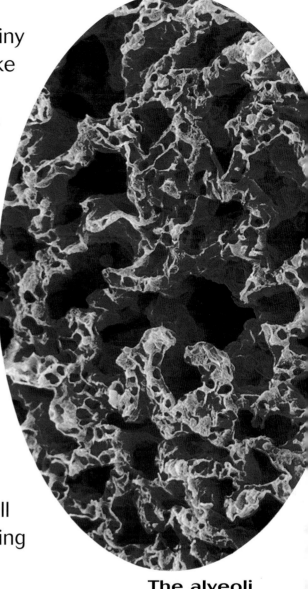

The alveoli in a lung.

Did you know?

Two special types of cells line your air passages. One type is covered in tiny hairs. The other makes slimy **mucus**. If you breathe in dust or **germs**, they stick to the mucus. Then the hairs push the mucus to the back of your throat. You swallow it and clear the germs away.

Water and waste

Your cells make waste as they work. If this waste stayed in your body, it would poison your cells. So your body has to get rid of it. You breathe out waste **carbon dioxide** (see page 21) during **respiration**. You get rid of waste food and waste water when you go to the toilet. These wastes come out of your body as **faeces** (see page 18) and **urine**. The amount of water in your body needs to be carefully balanced. If you take in more water than you need, your kidneys make urine to get rid of it.

The urinary system

Your kidneys and bladder are called your **urinary** system because they make and store urine. Your two kidneys are in your lower back. Your kidneys are like filters. Blood flows through your kidneys and they filter out water and other wastes. This liquid waste is called urine. Your bladder is like a stretchy bag. It stores the urine until you go to the toilet.

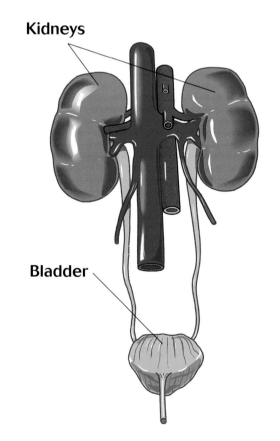

Kidneys

Bladder

The urinary system.

Filter system

Each of your kidneys contains more than a million tiny filters. Blood flows into your kidneys through your **renal artery**. Your kidneys filter and clean it. Then the blood flows out again through your renal **vein**.

The tiny filters inside a kidney.

Poison control

Your liver is the biggest organ in your body. It has several important jobs to do. Your blood carries your **digested** food to your liver. Your liver stores some of the goodness from the food. It also gets rid of some of the poisons in your food and drink.

Your senses

Your five senses are sight, hearing, smell, taste and touch. They tell you about the outside world. Each of your senses has a sense organ that is connected by **nerves** to your brain. Your five sense organs are your eyes, ears, nose, tongue and skin.

Eyes and seeing

You see things because light bounces off an object and goes into your eyes. The front of your eye **focuses** the light and passes it to the back of your eye. Here it makes an upside-down picture. Nerve cells send messages to your brain. Your brain sorts the messages and makes the picture you see.

Iris – the coloured part of your eye.

Pupil – light goes in here.

Lens – helps focus the picture.

Cornea – helps focus the picture.

Muscles – move your eye.

A cross-section of a human-eye.

Retina – nerve cells at the back of your eye.

Optic nerve – main nerve to your brain.

Did you know?

The special nerve cells in the back of your eyes are called rods and cones. You have about 120 million rod cells and 7 million cone cells in each eye. Rods can see black and white and different shades of light. Cones can see colours.

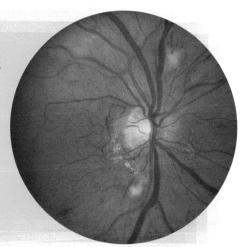

The human retina.

Ears and hearing

Your earflaps funnel sounds into your ear. They make your **eardrum vibrate**. Three tiny bones in your ear pick up the vibrations. As the bones vibrate, they make other parts of your ear vibrate too. Special nerve cells turn the vibrations into messages that travel to your brain. Your brain turns the messages into the sounds you hear.

Cells in your ears that pick up sounds.

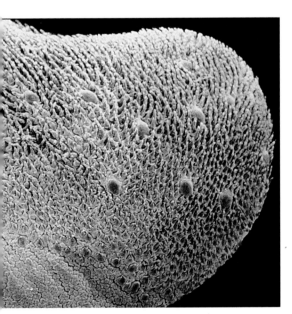

Taste buds on a tongue.

Taste and smell

You taste and smell things with your tongue and nose. Your tongue is covered in tiny taste buds. They are lined with special nerve cells that can taste sweet, salty, sour and bitter flavours. Smells are **chemicals** in the air. They float up your nose where nerve cells pick them up.

Skin and touch

Millions of nerve cells lie under your skin. Some sense heat and cold. Some sense light or heavy touch. Some tell you if things are hard, soft, rough or smooth. Some feel pain. Pain warns you that something is wrong with your body.

Brain and nerves

Your brain and **nerves** form your body's nervous system. Your nerves carry messages between your body and your brain. A thick bundle of nerves runs down your back. It is called your **spinal cord**. It is the main pathway between your brain and your body for the messages to travel along. Nerves branch off it to carry the messages all over your body.

Your amazing brain

Your brain controls every part of your body. Your brain is made of millions of nerve cells. Nerves carry messages about the outside world from your senses to your brain. Your brain sorts them out and then tells your body how to move, how to feel and what to think, see, hear, taste and smell.

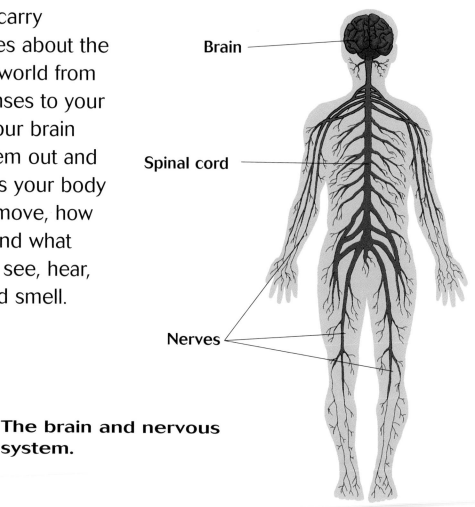

Brain

Spinal cord

Nerves

The brain and nervous system.

Nerve cells

Nerve cells are like long, thin wires. They carry messages in the form of electrical signals. You have about 100 billion (million million) nerve cells in your body. Some nerve cells carry messages from your senses to your brain. Some nerve cells carry messages from your brain to your muscles to make them move.

Speedy messages

All the time that you are awake, millions of nerve signals are whizzing around your body. Some signals travel at very high speeds, faster than a racing car. If you stub your toe, pain signals race from your foot to your brain. Then your brain quickly tells you to pull your foot away. When you are awake, about three million signals speed around your body every single second.

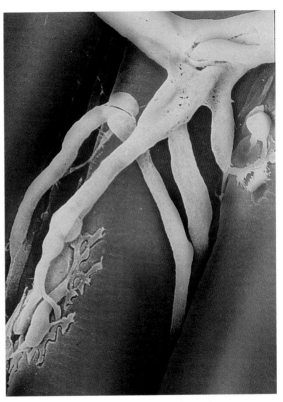
A nerve junction.

Did you know?
Some of your nerve cells will last your whole life but not all of them. Thousands of brain and nerve cells die every day. They can never be replaced or repaired. Luckily, you have millions more to go!

Reproduction

Reproduction means creating new life. You started life as two tiny cells – an egg cell from your mother and a sperm cell from your father. The two cells joined together to make a new cell. This new cell grew into a baby.

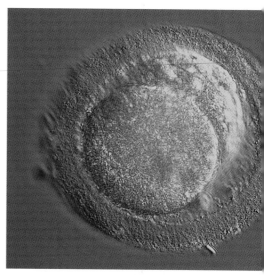

A new cell splits in two.

Reproductive systems

The parts of the body that make egg and sperm cells are called the reproductive systems. A girl's reproductive system usually starts working when she is about 11 to 13 years old. A boy's reproductive system usually starts working when he is about 12 to 14 years old.

Male and female

A baby grows when a sperm joins with an egg cell. This happens inside a female's body. Then the two cells make a new cell. The new cell splits in two, then four, then eight, until it forms a ball of cells. Over the next nine months, these cells grow into a baby.

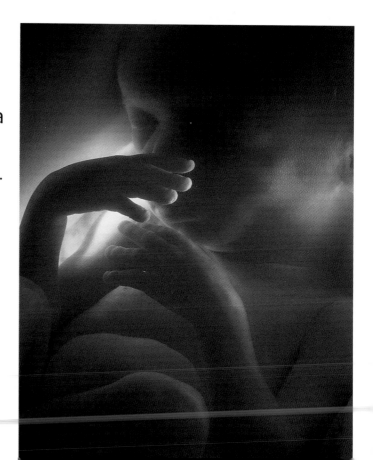

A baby growing inside its mother's body.

28

Boys or girls?

Your cells contain 46 tiny threads called chromosomes. These carry instructions, called genes, about what you will look like. You get half of your chromosomes from your mother, and half from your father. Two special chromosomes, called X and Y, decide if a baby will be a boy or a girl. All egg cells carry X chromosomes. Half the sperm carry X and half carry Y. An X and an X means a girl. An X and a Y means a boy.

Conclusion

Most cells are so tiny that you cannot see them. So it is hard to image that every living thing is made up of cells. Your own body is made of millions of cells. Without cells and the systems they build, you would not be able to move, eat food or read this book. Everything you do is down to your amazing cells.

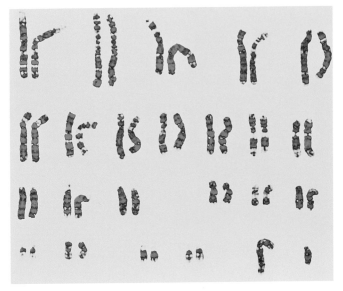

A boy's chromosomes.

Glossary

artery a blood vessel that carries blood from your heart

biceps muscles in your upper arm. They pull to bend your elbow.

bronchi two tubes in your chest that lead into your lungs

capillary the smallest blood vessel

carbon dioxide a gas that living things give out as waste during respiration

cartilage a rubbery material made from cells

cellulose a tough material in plant cell walls

chemical a subtance found as a gas, liquid or solid

chlorophyll green colouring found in plant cells. It helps the plant to make its own food.

chloroplast a tiny disc inside a plant cell. It contains chlorophyll.

circulatory means to flow round and round

clot to become lumpy and solid

cytoplasm watery jelly inside cells

digest, digestion to break food down into tiny enough pieces to pass into your blood

eardrum a membrane inside your ear. Sounds make it vibrate.

energy the power and goodness that living things need to keep their bodies working properly

evaporate to turn into gas. When water evaporates, it turns into a gas called water vapour.

faeces solid waste you pass when you go to the toilet

focus to make sharper and clearer

germ a tiny living thing that causes illnesses

haemoglobin a chemical in your blood that carries oxygen around your body

intestine a very long tube that is part of your digestive system

membrane a thin sheet of tissue

mineral a substance that helps to build your body and keep it healthy

mucus a sticky slime that helps protect the lining of your nose, lungs and stomach

nerve carries messages between the body and the brain

nucleus a tiny round speck inside a cell. It controls everything that happens in the cell.

oesophagus a large tube in your throat. It is used in digestion. It is also called your gullet.

organism a living thing

oxygen a gas in the air. Living things need to breathe in oxygen to stay alive.

ovule the female part of a plant

photosynthesis the way green plants make their own food from sunlight, carbon dioxide and water

plasma a watery liquid in blood. Blood cells float in it.

pollen tiny grains of powder that are the male parts of a plant

renal means to do with the kidneys

reproduce, reproduction to make new life

respiration the way oxygen is used by living things to make energy from food. Carbon dioxide and water are waste products.

saliva a liquid made in your mouth that helps to break down your food. It is also called spit.

sap the juices inside a plant that carry food and water

spinal cord a thick bundle of nerves running down your back, inside your spine or backbone

trachea a long tube in your throat. It is part of your respiratory system. It is also called your windpipe.

triceps muscles in your upper arm. They pull to straighten your arm.

urinary means to do with urine

urine waste liquid which comes out of your body when you go to the toilet

vacuole a space inside a cell

vein a blood vessel that carries blood to your heart

vibrate to shake or wobble

Index